1

Steve Malmude was born in Manhattan in 1940. He has published three books and two pamphlets of poems. He lives with his wife, Christine, in Limerick, Maine.

Miles Champion was born in Nottingham in 1968. He lives with his wife and children in Brooklyn, New York.

Red
Carpet

Steve
Malmude

edited by
Miles
Champion

CARCANET

First published in Great Britain in 2025 by
Carcanet
Main Library, The University of Manchester
Oxford Road, Manchester, M13 9PP
www.carcanet.co.uk

A CIP catalogue record for this book is
available from the British Library.

ISBN 978 1 80017 497 9

Book design by Andrew Latimer, Carcanet
Typesetting by LiteBook Prepress Services
Printed in Great Britain by SRP Ltd, Exeter, Devon

The publisher acknowledges financial
assistance from Arts Council England.

ACKNOWLEDGEMENTS

Some of these poems first appeared in *Catting* (New York: Adventures in Poetry, 1972), *From Roses to Coal* (New York: Shell, 1980), *I Got to Know* (Briarcliff, NY: Goodbye Books, 1997), *The Bundle* (Honolulu: Subpress; New York: Goodbye, 2002) and *Lifeguard* (London: Distance No Object, 2023); in *The Best American Poetry 2002*, ed. Robert Creeley and David Lehman (New York: Scribner, 2002), *Like Musical Instruments: 83 Contemporary American Poets*, ed. Larry Fagin (Frankfort, KY: Broadstone Books, 2014) and *Out of This World: An Anthology of the St. Mark's Poetry Project 1966–1991*, ed. Anne Waldman (New York: Crown, 1991); and in *12th Street Rag*, *Adventures in Poetry*, *The Delineator*, *Gerry Mulligan*, *The Harris Review*, *The Hat*, *Lingo*, *o•blēk*, *PN Review*, *Sal Mimeo*, *Shiny*, *Sun*, *Telephone*, *this* and *The World*. Many thanks to Steve Malmude, Christine Sears, Nancy Kuhl and Gabby Colangelo for their essential help in the preparation of this book.

CONTENTS

for Christine
with love forever

SONNET

Her love's omnivorous. An owl's wing's
feather isn't quiet nor eider duck
down soft enough not to trip her bloom's chuck
shut completely on the King of Things.
But the barb, what reciprocity! springs
foremost among the very parts that suck
her trap's confection. Kiss by kissing fuck
unhalters all her meat, and carnage brings
them to a frenzy. Lymph, blood, scum, cream
spill, and though we shield our eyes, still must he
eviscerate himself in husbandry.
His mandibles are knitting on her seam;
his thorax curls and pulsates, wrenching free
no member, but his entrail; exit the bee.

TO MARIANNE MOORE

Fort Greene Park
is cooling my face.
It's snowing at night.
Here was my country's ark
when I was young and light.
I saw Battery Place
from a tall tree.

Marianne Moore,
this interlude
strengthens the pedigree
of my old neighborhood.
You were there
in tricorner and plume
when I shot the authentic cannons
near the Martyr's Tomb
of rising granite flutes.

Brooklyn's stale recruits
will shoulder sleds tomorrow,
will breast the volleys down the slopes
of Dead Man's Hill;
and my sorrow is the sorrow
of universal hope's
individual.

I could have followed you,
camped at your door,
like Rimbaud,
Marianne Moore.

RAPHAEL, FROM THE ALEUTIANS

A month
like a mop!

Then steam topples.
Drink the propellers.
Frost perches throughout
hair. Legs shove off. Par-
kas toboggan to meet relief.

This country
take-off we pile
after one blizzard, I
was shaking snowdrift,
and the plane was beating
our women like a doorman.

One welder was
inch
chorus girls only
writhing paper.

Now that our navy is unimportant
a Martian ambles across Juneau.

Make that Baby-
lonian letter-
shaped baby.

Sterilization is the Cadillac of birth control
methods. And abortion is the Vol-
kswagen.

Any
joy is adequate, 'parting
hero'.

Thousands of ketchup soaks later,
that boy siphoned the dew
as a ventriloquist.

THE GOAT MAN

The people
have voted
that he could be doled
like a cripple,
yet he'll go foraging,
his skin bloated
either from cold
or gorging.

He'll toddle
down the road
with, say,
an empty bottle
clinking between his tits
inside a bib-pouch he sewed
from flyaway
tarpaulin bits.

Or he'll ferret
in a hole,
his sou'wester
turning like a turret,
or he'll tie his shoelaces
and march upon the knoll,
his Winchester
cradled against his braces

like a Torah.
And on Sundays
he'll walk in town
palsied with bravura
among the people,

who quickly go their ways
or try to stare him down
as he looks up at the steeple.

He has two goats,
weaned at birth,
with rickets,
a dog that eats oats,
two hens that chisel
through ice to earth
and whose eggs are briquettes
of gristle.

Now those two goats,
nodding in hay beds,
pant in an aura
of flashlit motes.
Their eyelashes flutter
at changing heads,
as if before a
flashbulb and shutter.

Lumberjacks
killed his dog;
he appeared
with an axe.
They dragged him like
they drag a log;
his beard
was one spike.

The police
pinch his nape
and rip swatches

from his fleece.
They begin
sort of a rape.
One snatches
something sewn in:

jewels
tumble
out of a seam;
he pulls
away and knees
them as they stumble
after, scream-
ing for his keys.

Now he's game
and tortured
off his land and chased
out of his name,
below Bath,
south of Old Orchard,
where he's about-faced
into promulgating wrath.

Men say in my ear
that he hoards
partridges and quail
pickling in beer:
twenty-nine kegs.
The marshal aborts
and offers for sale
these retrograde eggs.

He's jailed, dejailed.
I watch him kick in
his ruined door,
which someone has nailed.
He edges around
the bald chickens
thawing on the floor,
the goats in a mound

on a stage of mats,
refrigerating, moist
with mildew speckles
and the droppings of bats.
The ceiling is swollen,
there's a loose joist;
his collection of nickels
and guns is stolen.

MOONLIGHTING

I have another drunk in
me but not another comeback.
I want the sighs from
the top layer but I

am a lifeguard in addition
to working nights on this
waterfront carrying boxes of fruit.
A commission would enable me

reproductive life in them. But
you must call the Yukon.
The oldest war babies still
have eleven years of reproductive

life. The Gulf of Mexico
is the diaper of the
continent and the Great Lakes
are full of pigtail fluid.

ABELARD

I am a leech;
I am a bowel;
I am a screech
owl.

Save
me from sinecure!
I don't shave
below my tonsure.

Heloise,
they cut off my goods.
I can't see the trees
for the woods.

I can't see your thighs
for our shorn hair.
I can't exercise
despair

like a hunting dog.
Leaves
cover the Decalogue.
I'm wearing out my sleeves

on the granite table.
You are the more
capable
administrator.

TITLE AT THE END

Sports shirts
baked in the chaparrals,
and the orchards
baked the crab apples.

Lynxes slip,
oh heartbreaker!
Don't outstrip
us on our acre!

Adhesion
of a squirrel
to a television
aerial.

Scarecrows
tugged a leash
of fire hose
that didn't reach.

The title is the land
of desultory
quails, firebrand
poultry.

House
drowse
dry
goodbyeartist
Harknesscomplain
circumstances   coldertrain
glancesenjoinshouldrebraille
coinwheel   failseat
feelaisle   feet
eyeleveltrack
backward
cordpullit
walletunborn
sunburn

DANANG

The system shouts
a phoneme.
Phraze-yard
touts
hazard
an acronym

for DMZ
but it's 'demise'
or 'dooms'.
Such whimsy
booms
our marihuana highs,

whoreson
mother-of-pearl
fetishes.
But Thorazine
re-etches
knurl

on the handles.
A troop shuffle
destroys
the mandalas
of our stories.
Bivouac oval

recurs:
new bases'
wriggling
loudspeakers'

rigging;
oasis

particulars;
the intercom
transmits the burbles
of the water coolers;
the portables
succumb

to interference,
mucking
an aural
clearance.
As for our morale,
it's bucking

peace offers
which cloy
women's pity.
A soldier suffers
every city
but Hanoi,

resigned
to that outré
sort of tact
one shows the blind.
There is the pact
of dismay,

the nuisance
congratulations,
the Honolulu marriage

of insouciance
with air age
impatience;

then quiet:
it enters in
dispatches;
recondite
pencil scratches
on onionskin

distance
the comradery.
Someone leaves to shower
dentist's hands'
pinkness and power
into his body,

shedding his *Brattleboro*
Vermont
News,
which no one may borrow,
and whose
account

of early frost
sanctions hope
of knuckles bitten
and fingers crossed
in a mitten.
Envelope

glue on his spit,
a Fauve

works a sketch
around the slit
he cannot stretch
the hymen of.

He draws woodpeckers
smoking cigales,
copies cartoon characters
in lacquers
on Amtrak doors
from decals

on the gimmick
vorpal
plastic rifle butt
trying to mimic
walnut.
Rains topple

the terminal
men's room masonry
and slake
the urinal
camphor cake.
The visionary

builds his stasis
around some token,
afraid
eyeglasses
wormed from Medicaid
will get broken

to uncork
a tunnel,
where he'll find
pork
rind.
Their funnel

was last attack's
dud grenade
caul.
Their backs
tamped a wall
to suede.

It's like a boot
with loose
laces.
A tree's root
races
and thews

earth.
You bayonet
tarps, un-wad
each berth-
marinade,
vinaigrette-

claustral
with gas.
Then tanks
break muster, rowel,
trailing hanks
of grass.

Their tunnel
belches
and closes.
Our sentinel
exposes
the villagers.

A turret
aims
a cool
trial squirt.
A duck pool
flames,

slack
laser beam
probes eclipse
fire burning back
on the line of drips.
Crates of candy bars redeem

our stooges.
They harangue
the problem
refugees.
An antebellum
Danang

shill
tongues
his bullhorn.
Engineers shrill
over an aileron
and three bucket prongs

of a bulldozer.
Chinooks yank
our squads
away, over the dowzer
nods
of a tank.

LUCY,

I remember when Joanne
began to like her tea.

I'm useless without her body,
a shaken thermometer.

Lucifer, her body

is as warm
as her tongue, her nose

as precious
as a grapefruit spoon.

SUSIE,

I think of Webster, the subtle way
he's being reduced as a person.

Flabby,
thrilled Americans

flowers
with a rag content

preserves
in a balcony situation

quilted toilet
brush holders

adoption
sunglasses

phased
clothes

the bean supper the
potluck supper yes

you are fooling yourself
at a fashion college in Switzerland.

STOVE & LAMP

I stoke
or damp
still, the smoke
seeks out the lamp

climbs in the shade.
My tongue
touches the blade
of song.

I could cry.
My crowned
eye
gently comes round

an ash
lands on the sofa
I watch
the coffee.

BLUE TREE

I stood
like a blue tree
early in the morning.
The stores were locked about me,

the ghosts of women
tugging at my sleeve;
a smile showed in the foliage
which Joe says he won't shave.

And street lights
were switching off themselves,
the few stars
doing slow dissolves;

ghosts of women
at doors of post offices
were asking me,
slit for letters, this?

MAGI

You're different today
and your shoulders are beautiful
though there's nothing different in that.
Time stands still

when I'm with you.
How we used to disobey
the traffic lights on Second Avenue.
Pretty dim now aren't they.

I spent fifteen years
trying to learn a change of pace
and at the end of my career
that's all I had left.

As the two reached a corner
a walk sign lit up. See
the other old-timer chuckled
they're still afraid to pitch to me.

RUMORESQUE

Letters are coming through
with open envelope and no stamp,
and they are damp
with postage dew.

They come from a forest
of Maine or Oregon,
where Cupid took a hand in roadbuilding
or became the village priest.

They tell of children born
too cute for wards
and fathers running towards
the only place they have Toronto.

Mothers wait in uniform,
their names embroidered over one tit,
never mind that, how do you like it,
and what will you name the other one.

MORNING

Milton coyly breaks away
and goes the refrigerator.
We can't wait all night or day.
That makes you first on my list.

But now he is here
please enclose the next thing.
Harold do you care
about the picture.

The streets are empty, not a car
is in my way and I am free
to think of you and how you are
at home and in security.

Frank hops out of bed
puts on a bathrobe
and stands before an open window
with his father's arm around his shoulders.

ELISABETH,

Joe E. Lewis says
he went on a diet.
In fourteen days
he lost two weeks.

And I'm grown
vindictive, heavy,
knowing none
lives up to envy.

I will go visiting
a woman's rooms of wood
but not soliciting,
barely being understood.

O, the communes climb
across the prairie
with New Testaments
and no testaments.

CATTING

1.

Both crash in
and embrace,
to unfasten
each other's bras!

Oh traipse
with my blood
on your napes
from my shaving cut!

Scud
of nacre!
Am I a stud
or a wigmaker?

Am I a Mormon
or a skin grafter?
I love a woman
more after.

They hollered
from the cervix.
They tolerate
my first quickies.

I bandage
tied hair.
I manage
where.

2.

They shop
for their husbands,
they swap
fine commands

of whole
magazines:
role,
means,

settle
up, down,
like nettle,
like swansdown.

Good enough
and par.
Shotgunned off,
prodded far,

and still the hive
balloons in the casement.
Sweet saliva
hardens to cement.

Careers
attend kindergarten.
A terrier's
hard-on.

Brahinsky
born 1884
Province of
Tchernigov.

Emigrated to London 1904
and a year later America.
Died in New York 1953.
I Have My Mother's Black Hair

I have my mother's black hair and green eyes
And my father's hands, delicate, thin,
And my blood sings and seethes within
The blood of my grandfathers, Jews who lived on the Dnieper.

And on my head are nights spent with my comrades
Yearning for the tender joys of life.
And I have the teeth marks on my breast
Of my shy and sheltered wife.

GOOD

If Groundhog Day be fair and bright
then winter will take another flight, but if
Groundhog Day be dark and gray
the worst of winter has passed away.

It is very quiet here in Parsonsfield,
there don't seem to be any laws passing,
only people going to their work and back;
it does seem as though everybody is gone.

It looks like spring but it's so quiet I don't see
any children out to play, don't hear much.
There aren't many autos passing now
but only people going to their work.

You know what Martin Luther said,
if the world were going to end tomorrow
I would still plant my little apple tree,
especially if the world were going to end tomorrow.

TRUANT

Any
fire has more
poignancy
to a smoker

cafés
with the densest
relays
of audiences

spelunking
a very stretched
Slinky
with a peacock plume

the moon
falls in place
and seats
process men

and
water bugs
read my mind
like quarterbacks

what is lost
will return
with the luster
of being foreign

angora
interlude
in the pedigree
of a neighborhood

the power
of daydreams
beyond oh
curl up with me in book form

THROUGH ELODEA

I stand
watching minnows
debride my oozing
hatchet wound

the pines
throw their pollens
for the trees
of centuries

by the frogs' strong
incantation
from expanding
neck skin

I wade
in the lake
shallows I walk
through elodea

PIERO HELICZER

He raises
carrots
in a plastic
bin, and chives, and
beans.
              And in one film
I heard his maintenance
of the squeak-
ings from the fingering
of a guitar.
              I said
              to him:
              You love
              the
              delicate
              things
              that are too
              easy
              for me to
              disregard.
              And he said:
I myself am
delicate.
              And I
              think I
              understand
              him and why
              Jack Smith kept
              him and then bashed
              in his cello and threw
              him out.

THE HIGH TIDE

She has a bane.
Fish, see her again.
  I can't stop prais–
I think about her ways.

  My liberated hand is smeared.
A Greek, bright as a slug. Wearing
  the village road or wrapped in
a V-black dress . . .

            Once again room where an, an;
    dawn sickens me. Heavy wings dice and knuckle.
Angel! angel and playina! A gagged aorta,
    a light prison, a field of azure-tinted wheat.

A loud
sound.

      Everything is sweet.
A crook as well aor.
A crook as well air.

RADRIATIC

I'm into touring. I spurn
and hate this squealing area.
Right inside me the wards turn.
I have known the ulterior

vibrations and the short jerks
switching their tails behind them
like alley cats watching fireworks.
I throw things away to find them.

Friendships flabby from double adultery,
and smoke pulling the front teeth
like Turkish taffy. It's not ribaldry;
it's like hydraulics underneath

and pumps down in the hold.
Oh I shock my heart's desire
once in a while: the lolled
urethra breaks into a higher

falsetto, organs secrete glue;
then we deal, being sordid: tool!
That's my experience, and in a few
hours I hunt my fellow fool.

That one who cut me bangs,
she was my get-off gal. I
don't know where she hangs
around now or with that guy . . .

She said I could not judge
her grasp by a brace of flirts.
I told her not to budge
till I ran out of spurts.

Beauties might steal care of me
from her. Same-day flesh and blood,
that need not know to love me,
might like me for a stud.

Night commerce makes St. Mark's
Place a humidor. And I enjoy
tensing under the mercury arcs
in the parks. Exhausts buoy

the neons; they glint like the sardines
in the old James Brown's pompadour.
So I cruised in my hardiness,
but she found the subway fodder.

She jumped to get us from there
and find Lucy and Crony
Tony have the influence to spare
us bits of coast, of a balcony

cantilevered like a surfboard
from a vanguard of sand;
establishments which monitored
the surfers like a grandstand

got wrecked to pieces. Up the ragged
Massachusetts coast, the hurdle
where Ted Kennedy's steering wheel raked
over his lap like a souped-up turtle.

Soon I was trudging over broken
apples. It really takes a smart fish
to live on bait. The frog stops croaking;
it doesn't mean that he will splash.

The country nights are colder;
that disturbs me, for I never sleep.
I feel her temple, and my shoulder
bumps it in the heatless Jeep.

I have to readjust
the rearview mirror.
—My candle in the gust,
oh my shiverer,

Jo Brahinsky, you deserve
to ring in my ear
like an awful swerve
to avoid deer!

ROSS

Hey Ross, hey Ross
let the spoons get lost,
and don't worry, don't worry
on our anniversary.

Sometimes,
when the air is full of climbs,
or in the stillest seasons,
when the air is full of reasons

to give you up forever—
conifer, conifer,
golden rods
and the pods

of the milky weeds
and their silk seeds;
rural, rural,
the universe is in a whorl,

and we're clinging, clinging
to the earth's crust, singing
to each other:
me, you, Connie, Ahab, and my brother.

I CAME WALKING

I came walking with
this sweater on,
after a lady with
her hair in a bun;

I gained and gained on her.
At 11th Street
I could watch
her heel mint a shit.
But then off she went,
kicking back the edges of her coat's vent.

I forgot St.
Mark's Church, where Jim
was reading, and Harris
was replacing him

at the door
with the plastic bucket.
I
passed the church by, for by a clock it
was a time
when a reading may be over,

and I am
to hover
or go
on the portico.

LEAFLET

Farmer of Song Ve Valley,
if this map represents
the land you live on,
go with your family
to Nghia Hanh,
a hamlet of tents

and not one grave.
You will receive rice
and medical care.
At Nghia Hanh you will be safe.
Your missing son is there.
You will renew old ties.

The soldier who handed you this
is here to free you from the Vietcong
and North Vietnamese invaders,
who bring upon you the ravages
of war. Go with our aviators
to prosperous Nghia Hanh, where the GVN is strong

and ready to protect you. You will recapture
your peaceful life. You will escape fear
for the lives of your loved ones, and your daughter will marry.
If you want to go to Nghia Hanh by helicopter
you will be able to take only what you can carry.
But Nghia Hanh is very near

by helicopter. If you desire to go to Nghia Hanh,
touch the soldier on the back of his hand.
Then he will know, and you will be safe.
Follow the instructions of the American.
If you do not want to leave, tear this leaflet in half,
now, in front of him, and he will understand.

CHURCHES DWINDLE

We are quiet and pale
canopy and a veil
you are under a tapestry rich
and heavy as chain mail

I am big as a cloud
baby bellows out loud
Grandma spoons her gruel from a dish
we are simple and proud

We are tender and soft
blouse and collar are soft
you are holding baby close
and I am working aloft

I am the last to bed
halos around my head
I beg you not to be morose
but smile and be happy instead

POEM FOR MY WOODBURNING STOVE

Goodbye to you!
Freezings and thaws
got to me like applause.
I gave you my shoes

which were velvety twos.
It was grate. Joanne
used every shape of pan,
we swam in flan,

corn and oysters in cream
and split-pea soup, oh real!
We can't remember the meal
but we recall the asylum.

I'd say we fried a thousand eggs
with your heat on our legs
and rising up the flue
melting snowflakes.

Pleasamay   ingredientheir   powening
chasintook,   chasultook   gincorner
pridou   fowhe   gommon   endfriend
materialou,   rufflerange.

YOU READ

You have abstraction, the major
weakness.

      And you have Keats's sure
apprehension,
   signifying suspense.

            You have

his sense of the hero of Italy.

And you have a scene with C. M. Bowra
reminding you of the Boccaccio story.

HOW I COMPOSE

Librarians
lie on sofas
in the ladies' room.
And there is something about the lighting

the lights dim as the conductor raises his baton
conduct is still at issue the conduct of writing
and the enormous friendship of husbands.
Someone I admire

wrote a great pile
of French prose
for exercise.
Scrapbooks served me

and staring at
my typed material.
Not doing anything
has served me.

RAY O VAC

Why
moon
over my
persona

the shine
is soon
taken
off that

character
is what
I am
in the dark

the
nearest
must
hold the candle

farther
away
falsely
still

allure
through
shine
alone

airborne
carbon
paper
square

starve
the conditioner
of
air

tiny
flyaway
hermetic
gesture

always
blows
down
a main line

THE PIER GOING BETWEEN

What do you think are your big
problems now Mr. Smith? What
is your biggest problem?

—Masturbation.

Any other problems besides that?

—Drinking too much tea.

Why is that a problem do you think?

—Why, I have the wrong body, the wrong
song and the wrong person.

Did that happen how did that come about?

—The pier.

The pier?

—The pier going between.

ST. ELMO, ILLINOIS

The process of gesta-
There is no question
of living in rebell-
ion again. And we feel
nervous and physical.

One partner alone.
Problem: My husba-
Solution: The understa-
tement of the year!

Terrifyingly
defective children, children
too close together, fewer and better children.

I'd like to write a song about
    innocent, randy times

and date a victim of selfishness.

SEE HOW QUIETLY I CALL YOU

Small garden
audience of breaths
I developed
in the fifties and sixties.

My pride
was resolved
on the large side
and then swallowed.

Look at Calder
he's painting planes now
see how quietly I call you
when I wonder where you are.

I call you by disappearing
down peculiar alleys
with inferiors
who will not find humor in this.

NO, I'M NOT ANXIOUS

No, I'm not anxious
about how
the public and critics
react to me now.

They have discovered
I am a Greek citizen.
No, Canada,
I say in a thick accent.

I know the pointless
epigrams
of people in agreement
and control.

Like King Henry's fifth,
the youngest and called
most beautiful,
I'm lonely and appalled.

TO PORTLAND

At night I see the gas
station settling on a lily.
The vegetables stand motionless,
the molehills and badgered earth
under the moon's wig-exactness.

I know the gossamer
breakaway the dogs make
chasing the locomotive.
And by midnight,
one chimney star,

bathroom door
ajar, gore,
mousery
(the spider
webs across the menses of the mice).

Between a stone
floor and the crab
nebulae, do you
see the bolts
of blue ribbons?

I see the terrier
and the tangled spindle
and the tuft of lint
and the drains gulping
like barnacles.

And throughout the storm
I saw a mountain
laden with a rag.
I saw the rain stream
pulling the horses' heads down

like reins. I saw into the doorway
from the sun. I saw
the grass beneath your chair,
a faded square
of green.

And I have seen you peeing on the axe;
I saw your cunt,
like Joe Louis bowing,
coaxing everything;
my binoculars are down. But

don't you see
the tankers, tending
and slalom-
ing, and don't
you see the frescoed

banana and the
shaggy
forces
of the diesels . . . ? at least
the emptiness of the pharmacy?

Recessive cobble-
stones, the stoops, like

irregular verbs, the
dwindling statue
of Longfellow. I enjoy

the table
of our
country's
contents;
houses

in a series,
transportation, gentle
random, brute
idols of
shipping,

o beaten-
back jumbo jets; ads, gray
art room,
dough
in the Atlantic Ocean, and

the turnstiles of wind . . . !
Frequency,
not a promise;
the accosting
flexibility.

Centipede upon
the toothbrush.
And now new sack
cement, materials
in niches like empyrean eagles.

A squirt of pigeon stool
like the backbone of a herring.
The helping, the apartheid of the legs;
the men stand akin to relief,
and the main beam is a wiving thing.

Prostrate, penetrated annoyance;
a boy blunders out of EMERGENCY
with gladiolas.
(Short legs bulged
like mixing spoons;

a dwarf's
slingshot-like white
coat, a hunchback's
with its pressure area.) Across,
a roofer humping along on leniency.

The sunlight on him
changes as ginger changes
intensity on the tongue. My
semen falling down in water
like a clown in pain.

Iron dogs say me and you
don't know the prices
of bleeding in a circle . . .
(Let your grandfather bathe
like elm wood wobbling on a lathe.)

Downtrodden
mayhem, marauding,
priming housewives. (Loose

breasts over a kettle, the shtetl, the Stoa,
MABSTOA, illness in uniform as in Krokodil.)

I wash my hands in holes
dug for the telephone poles.
. . . locomotive from Anchorage
Alaska convinces, badge
reindeer-catcher impresses . . .

Then I rode back
to Limerick where I saw
the cats stretched out reasoning.
I heard the lake's principal starts,
the Argyrol conkings-out and -in.

THE BUNDLE

The Torah
wanders
one day
it comes here

the wind
has pushed
the parachuted
bundle

that has been
bound
in twine
and abandoned

one day
I find a teenage
diary
in the garbage

the bundle
of paper
is a small
solid affair

I throw
the brick
through a Nordic
shopwindow

COMPANION POEMS

1.

Egging on the pus,
pitching its tight tents,
who sponsored this circus
inside of my pants?

No longer than to pee
I can hardly stand,
or ask for sympathy
with such a heavy hand.

She likes it in the tub
with me, except today;
I give her back a scrub,
she really turns away!

I limp to bed aware
of the way she combs
out her wet hair
in the other rooms.

2.

She has hooded eyelids,
her face is sharp;
a knife among squids
and among carp.

Whoever wharves
at her fins
my love carves,
my love entertains,

without a salver,
without watercress;
my love is silver
under the dress.

My love is not a girl
smiling at rain.
She's a pickerel
in a sewer main.

I WAS IN THE APARTMENT

I was in the apartment
but the woman I won't part with
was on queer street
I was on my feet

I will stay
oh gray
eyes pink and numb
nipples like the thumb

of Nathan's oyster
vendor I will hoist her
to me through your hair
don't remain down in a chair

tilting the honest nipple
and the imponderable
eye
at me say goodbye

'Clubs' and 'Men's'

The program and ticket impulse is everywhere.
A program should whisper of widespread interest.
A hive, producing casual write-ups and car stickers,
should lure the unexpected element.
The friends and parents of the performers
give them anklets of colored sealing and leaf-
like stickers of paraffin for their cheeks.

THE PRODU The Production

You begin the stage of wanting
and blending. You may catch
the library fires in reflectors.
Your storyline, if you have got one,
should be loosely but fully followed. The dancing
sources rise, a hostess group to the imagination,
kinks dance around the bodies' privates . . .

Lily

Willow

Moths start tagging the lighting.
Strive for the deep crepey effect
for yourself but let your cardboard equal
be dedicated to stripes. The feet are
'rubber tips'. Your Pan wears no eye
and chest harnesses. They are appropriate
to the turtles. Your wig should be the snug
light-green top of the adhesive-taped melon.

Turtle

But it is worn rakishly. Banana oil
should be applied around the eyes four.
The beak is tied shut in a snore,
and the nostrils are finished
around with a fixative.
Two shiny tin cans
fit the thighs, the groin
appears sharply defined.

MUSIC
The Selection of Music

Keep your gummed side to the accompanist. Take
the islands of monastic interest
into account.

How to Make Magic Flame

This is how the Carroll Club pool did it:
They revived ancient memory fires,
they disguised the scheme of lights as a lumber item,
they backlit
a Bloody Mary.

End of Spectators' Pl

You have the walk of the pool.
Its columns may be propelled
from the curb of the pool.
Flatter

their inboard need
for swimming
until
the water has raised a shoulder.

        Blo

Flat-bottom rowboats filled
with the safety of persons
bob at anchor close by.

MONTVILLE

Once I had
a beautiful girl
and she made me
a primary color.

Then she picked flesh
from the Crayolas
and I reflected
with closed eyes.

Pick apples in the sun
make hay or hoe corn
then go in and shut
your eyes and press them with

your hand. You shall still see
apples hanging in the bright light
with boughs and leaves or the
tossed grass or the corn flags.

CONRAD,

I want to walk
because someone
left spots in New York
I get rusty on.

I don't want to die
because that would be
like taking Gandhi
from a baby.

I want to
satisfy something
in a toy store milieu
on Thanksgiving morning

because
Lee Merriwether says
some characters from Christmas
have crossed holidays.

NOVELTY ABBEY

Oliver invited me
to stay with him
at his country home
Novelty Abbey

a harvest brought in
by delicate hands
raised the hairs
all down me

a quiet roommate
helped pay the bill
and so our circle
was complete

but a bitter feast
is steaming hot
and a mouth must
be found to eat

HONORIFIC

Mail
rain
opal
stain

a
bare
blue
cyclorama

rabbi
eye
akin
to ink

ribbon
placed
within
lace

and a
discreet
banana
seed

marionette
linoleum
gym
mat

archly
invent
each
instant

bank
on an
array
of midwives

at low
tide
after your
period

ivory
owes you
its fine
grain

gloom
breeds
presumed
readers

Silver
Latin
mandolin
ensembles

honorific
before a
brick
camera

in front
of that
ribbon
of dust

bicycle
seats'
theatrical
height

arms
swing
summer
and winter

now
only a
hay leaf
is left over

Sunday
wind
Bourbon
appreciation

flint
bring back
scent
of tobacco

dateless
fillers
insiders'
follies

quicksand
foot powder
Bermuda
twang

I use
and mention
a neutral
twinge

formula
for foliage
symbol
for skin

moon aura
so boring
menorah
sobering

I laid
my head
on pillows
tears oozed

a car
cut in two
to allow
for camera work

what
punches in
then swirls out
abdicating

wing tip
stakes down
the vortex
of farmland

the decor
and spectacle
like a tilted
decal

I meant
to soften
my complaint
not press it often

the Adams
Jefferson
might have been
postage stamps

The Sacred Wood
was published
it was valid
and noble

sorrow
has failed to
become the metaphor
for my frailty

as if
chess pieces
themselves sniffle
and clean their pipes

constructions
of ordinary tact
cornerstone
of disenchantment

a dollar bill
as a bookmark
in a paperback
Wings of the Dove

women I track
from their youth
stand off flat
and make vistas

probity
has burned my covers
to kill a flea
and made me hers

the steel
looks like it's floating
so the bamboo
looks fine on it

I'm going upstairs
to steal some shellac
stars
twinkle congested

there are photos
with wolves playing
like snowbirds
on the ash bank

and outrage
as a neglected
guard might stage
remnants of an attack

look at my background
more holes than wool
and here I stand
warm and wonderful

her tight coat
makes it easier for her
to walk down the stairs
and not be drowsy

FLOWERS & KEYS

What have you done
O cluster of friends
turned the breezes away
for a surprise package?

And disappointments
aren't they the lepers
with the spirit
to welcome each other.

Spring is no longer
Henry David Thoreau's
favorite season. Yes
beware of enterprises

that require new clothes.
And the way you dress
nobody realizes
you have lost the title.

FROM ROSES TO COAL

You could have the pair
of hands that always waits
with oil from somewhere
between the license plates.

Look at the moon.
I have never seen
such an old man
wearing jeans.

I don't have to look,
she answered
with a beautiful turn
of the apron,

that's the curiosity.
Then the pantry,
the half-door, the whole
went from roses to coal.

The leaves are like girls
in the Scout program
and the frogs are singing
by the garage beauty shop.

A lake touching me
like paper cup wine.
From my aluminum canoe
the rainbow seems to lead to a Canadian surgeon.

SUB

Full
dress
mutual
faithfulness

skipped
delighted
to her
bureau

only
a bundle
under
control

those
solving
fingers
of hers

yearned
for money
to buy
style

her
painter
was there
I hadn't

seen
him yet
just his
coat

eliminate
dirt
and laugh
at it

emphasized
words
pierced
my doze

I was
asked in
to examine
and use

existing
joists
particularly
on a pergola

I used
coins
as decision
machines

I imputed
forgetful
zeal
to poets

autumn
air
to stir
the memory

I
scarcely
turned
a hand

LET ALONE ACQUIRE

You open
the safe
and begin
the day

peel
citrus
and feel
it in your face

expel
a tracer
of internal
atmosphere

choose
how openly
intrusive
you'll be

it
is quarter to eight
or twenty
to nine

you
slip out
of a shower
for the shampoo

girl in
lobby talks
to doorman
snow on dogs

water
at orgy
temperature
at the St. George

once
real
damage is done
quietness won't heal

it used to
be furtive
in a booth
in De Robertis

it ends
with a hostess
pretending
to be asleep

slam
more
like a car door
than a garbage can lid

put
the receiver
in a boot
in the refrigerator

with love
permanently
in all novelty
and lameness

mood
I can't contain
shrewd
stroke of installation

a secret
that undermines
character
not merely plans

where
evidence
is hard to imagine
let alone acquire

TAKE

Take
everything
you like
with you

into
the blue
metal of the
shutter

inner
ring
going
to the outer

who will
feel
me down
to the ground

KRAZY

A whole life
you've
drawn
in

and
red
as a skinned
rabbit

on my black
bike
I've set
out

brick
pink
and marine
green

security
guard
in the
foyer

stereo
doing
soaring
for you

HOBOKEN

If Hoboken
had a ferry
I'd sink
roots here

the father
of athletics
is a faceted
figure

loosely
connected
to the Kool
Jazz Festival

the library
is open
nonjudgmental
free

in a carrel
of the library
I see
Carol

her famous
yawn
is territorial
display

A PARKING

space
I leave
closes
by itself

this
slight
push is
almighty

my
curiosity
is all
alive

the hot
penny
cuts
its way

DUCHESS

If the ease
you take with me isn't thorough
why it's base.
I know what it's worth

if you can write
Words for the Wind say
and your friends still call you Ted.
I feel like a boy

when she has fun without me.
What very shy man
ever paraded around New York City
without a reason

a maiden in her flower?
Or a ballerina in her first role
with Balanchine himself
as Polio.

CROSSING DEERING OAKS PARK

I draw my snow cap off
so you can see my age
for I have walked enough
in youthful camouflage

Out of range or charter
my vanity still falls
well within my character
for citing intervals

Muted rose aviator jacket
I had a lean hard body
that was soaked with sweat
dozens of times a day

Now that the sewing machine
has white thread in it
the shroud around my station
is stitched even tighter

1980

Every
year
brings
a keyring

tool
bits
stored
in carousel

soft
dangle
get sucked
in by yourself

heat
from chimneys
wiggles
atmosphere

potential
memorial
maintenance
systems

embrace
a volunteer
dune grass
planter

bashful
using
old-fashioned
yours trulys

so the
pitched and
combined
diverbs go

from a thin
party line
to a rich
premonition

ma
tell me
how the wine
got on the curtain

arguing
in the spring
the cry
of guarantee

the cross-
word puzzle
overlap
of property

there are
garage doors
on the backs
of trucks

the rule
of suction
Goya's *Burial
of the Sardine*

in the middle
of a saucer
lower than all
horizons

I am a parachute
touching down
like a cut
diamond

soft sigh
thank you sound
wants me to be
Canadian

a canoe
with a rainbow
going out
to a license plate

loving-kindness
over credulity
the Aquarians
are like that

intelligently
helpful
and hindering
gel columns

improve
on newcomer
illusions of
being elsewhere

generating a
fleeting little group
that takes away
riches in a cab

the double dais
of celebrities
from both coasts
delaminates

humid afternoons
in the exercise room
swelling like a
rusk in tea

Stevens Institute
has sports facilities
the people use
on the q.t.

I move my head
from side to side
so I can see
through the Nautilus

THE PASTURES

Here are
the forests
leafless
and bare

the wide
brown
fields wet
with rain

I still
see your land
as the jewel
in the lane

I see
the green
grass frozen
in the ice

become
a Southern
theme
town

once
I was
in a famous
place

built
in
devotion
and revolt

there used to be
a missionary
aspect
to it

the dry
hemisphere
broadcast
into the wet

there was
a lap
of tangled
yarn

accorded
entry
into the
horizon

a pasture
that a beast
can sense
lies ahead

precision
soaks away
into the one
sheer beauty

a historic
house
built
of bottles

an after-
coming head
between the bucket
seats of a car

it makes no
mind no how
America's
cup is there

I can see it
move across
the network
in real time

primitive
weather vanes
have
bullet holes in them

the skies are
leaden on one
side radiant
on the other

some realist
painter's vast
estate stretches
all about

if it were a farm
and he were a friend
it would confer an
axial sense on me

VISITED

Some
form
of rough
justice

as
troubled
areas
rebuild

and
I remain
present
as a workman

all
silence
and flannel
softness

PALATIAL SUM

I flirt
with the possibility
of having to clean out
my closet

but my closet
is as big as my beat
and I am the skeleton
that lives in it

my apartment
is so small
I have to go out in the hall
to change my mind

anyone
can navigate my apartment
just by speaking into
their telephone

PARAGON

You stay
black against night
and white
against day

behind drapes
four hours
on all fours
down fire escapes

a radio
in a kitchen
an outhouse
among pigs and animation

have you ever
been in a room
where every bed
had shoes on

giving
useless advice
the privilege
of one who is off duty

the flashlight
a maintenance man
leaves on
in his back pocket

hustlers'
Popeye
mopping
muscles

you eat
water
from the bedsprings and dates
from the calendar

the second stories
are drying off
and the bar door is
in a huff

paintbrushes
bathe together
and bathe the bruises
of blind goats

gather sap
any day it runs
take the nap
you've wanted all along

the result
is you're not sleeping
a bureau takes root
in your fantasy

you've commissioned
one of your
specially trained
heraldic artists

and dark
purpose and chance
frank your elegance
like a postmark

despair and hope
follow you home
the smell of soap
will make you come

down a ladder
so carefully it wobbles
your father
in a bathrobe

the perfume
stewardesses lay so thin
boy with soap on him
like a lemur

blue Standard
washes you away
thou sands of your self
without a hair astray

you've disciplined
gramercy with lack
grame and the wind
remember your back

you were intelligent to-
night but this made-
up life the muted
perversity of it

wedding pictures
the bride and groom
flirting on the hassocks
dancing in the room

Farancanteen
I order you to kneel
on hard dry beans
the letter F makes all fall

in modern funerals
a bier
is a little silver dolly
which resembles a baby carriage

look at each other
with dawning delight
and take the cover
off the typewriter

folk notion
of living near or far from here
disordering
effect of a failed departure

hefting the duffel
strenuously wanton or
yanking back on the double
doorknobs like oarsmen and

the wind catches words
and flings them across the street
my cap will take the curse
off this suit

roaches in crisp jackets
rustle in the bass speaker
a plane flies across
the windows like a fleur-de-lis

boots that beat the express train
and sometimes slip on tokens
might involve painted
toenails under heavy socks

your grandfather's
corduroy pants argued
like pinking shears
crossing the Williamsburg

God mixed up the builders' speech
in other words
he made some talk one language
and some another

I GOT TO KNOW

Spring rain
washes the arrow
out of the head
of the snowman

it is the sign
that our case
has been
diagnosed

one has
another day
to acquiesce
I got to know

my colognes
this morning
and they
got to know me

HABITAT

I see
Community
with its roofs
removed

I hear
its voice
from everywhere
in the house

but it engages
me less
than Joey Bag
of Donuts

that small
contractor
who is all
up in there

GROVER

Jim
Henson's
hidden
hands

some
hothouse
holds
them

never
more
rely
on me

that
little
dust
blossom

WHERE I GO

I go down
to the Pueblo
it is unmistakably
my destination

all these second
chances going around
but they are long
gone by then

or I abandon
the apartment
no destination
in mind

just a gone
feeling
with glittering
connections

MY OWN BRUSHES

Art literally
crushed
the Israelites
in Egypt

however charged
with lead
my life took shape
with a job

I thought that
in my hard hat
kneeling in front
of a can of paint

for there are poets
who cannot drink
a queen held the ink
stone for Li Po

REGION

Sorrow
and
a narrow
mind

shear a
high
cherry
tree

fallen
away
what can
I say

o
snowy
Polish
region

unseen
beautiful
stone
wall

erase
me as
a social
animal

A WOODSHOP

I have
a silver
hair
on my sleeve

a drop
of glue
on the top
of my shoe

my cozy
woodshop
draws sharp
eyes ah

soon
my craft-bound
solitude
will end

NOTICE

Old	Those of us
people	who are older
living	we look each
young	other over
earnest	exchange ecstasy
as	among one another
Paradise	our eyes roll back
Lost	in rapture
veins	the pupils
stand	disappear
on	there are only
my hand	the blind whites
tears	when we get together
roll	the kids are gone
there	it's all over
also	it's the big one

I DROPPED IN ON HIM

After Mary
sublet her place to Jim
and moved in with me
I dropped in on him

we sat around
Mary's table
he paid me the rent
opened a bottle

told me a joke
about life in Woodstock
and read me the poem
from that time

when we were capable
of another
postwar culture
based on rent control

FAUNAL REMAINS

As
reverie
plus
moves me

away
from
the early
dream

toward
water
goal
of the animals

men
fall
into
a pool

after
being
faked into
the air

as
others
rise
seething

a tear
promises
the air
an ace

and I
devour
my
heroes

where
they
are
shy

G
forces
on my
face

THE ANARCHY

When the young
blood is
dying
to cut loose

the move
that takes them
out of frame
is love

and the spurious
freedom
of the empty
house

tells me
they receive
a centralized
directive

FASCINATION

The faith
I had
in the depth
of your mood

it was
so small
it was nothing
but trouble

to doubt
some part
is to
believe the rest

not
a bad start
and the road
is endless

THE SURPRISE BRONZE

If you open my book
there has been a mistake
it would be better
if you read the newspaper

the blind mother
the welder father
paying for the lessons
the surprise bronze

I picked up *The Web*
and the Rock again
the other day and
it held up very well

I have a question for you
what the hell happened
I see you around
what's your story

HERE'S THE KETTLE

Here's the Kettle
household
today ma's
in a jam

the kettle
of Brooklyn
was around as serious
as a courtroom

that quota
of consortium
contracting at home
to extend abroad

the shocking
moment when
I have to hand
this over to actors

CHEVRON

Dangerous
rig
exhausted
driver

come
victorious
from
the maze

whose
lured
captured
industries

prudently
enter
a dormant
hour

THRESHOLD

Put the key
in the door
said Ali's
corner

the fine
parade
goes by on
another street

hundreds
of standards
one after
the other

designs
in a carpet
trodden
underfoot

THE LITTLE DAUGHTERS

Little daughters
in the middle of the night
why are you not
asleep again yet?

The stomping ground
must always die down
and be
curtained away!

But we don't mind
being looked at
we like it!

We lie awake
for hours
with happiness actually.

APRIL

April
is
full
of movies

when
bohemia
is in
bloom

it
is
protected
by bees

let
them
do it
as a team

and art
for
art
is power

via
writing
all day
long

the price
for
this
power

is my
easy-
going
song

what
am I
afraid
to say

I can
curate
my own
art

the
art of
love
poetry

me
a boy
out
of the ghetto

isn't
art
a kind
of dirt

the man
is now
saying
no

PERFECT FRONT DOOR

My summer
is threadbare
these jeans
are chains

always
the sense
of the futility
of maintenance

yet I feel
the cool
night air
from the open door

capital
crosses the border
at will
why not labor

THE THREE GRACES

One poem
comes along
and puts them
onto a new thing

they summon
by the magnets
of its
construction

continuity
of outline
holding the three
into one

and once they're
embarked
all the ropes
start pulling

LINE

Poetry
as a dot
to stare at
in secret

my love
for brief
literary
utterances

crushed
by the weight
of this
regret

swollen
with the day's
line
as always

RELIEFS

Let us
be let
us do
business

it is
unclean
even
to notice

since
sight
is a genteel
sense

and
reliefs
tend
to reverse

BLARING

The thing
is to know whether
one another were
blaring

in a restaurant
setting
within hearing
of you name it

hopefully
which means humbly
you are into
a diminuendo

the idea say
of a café
as the meeting place
for misfits

RUSH HOUR

The evening
rush hour
is up in
the air

it is more
than a getaway
it is a
rapture

serious
and heartfelt
as humor
will allow

I am just
groping for
a variant
of this joke

the joke
has a little
theoretical
framework

I forget that
I'm not
supposed to
know

OVERWHELMING

Overwhelming
mental states
wipe out
the coping skills

of a naked
lactating goddess
and a dressed
he-man god

soon it's safe
to laugh out loud
manifestly
interested

laughter
that stifles
their signature
wordless vocals

RED CARPET

A name
they call me
in the bosom
of her family

caused me
to believe
I was her first
true love

looking into
her ways
then averting
my gaze

caused me
to believe
I was her first
true love

the illusion
of looking in on
a concealed
world

the story
of women laughing
as a boy
listens in

caused me
to believe
I was her first
true love

comfortable
face subject
on a pillow
folded back

the romantic
abasement
I hear about
and mock

caused me
to believe
I was her first
true love

I am not
absolute
she compares
me to others

a feeling
of mystic
superiority
supports me

so do I
says the leaf
falling off
so do we

say the
withered
arms and necks
of Lake Sokokis

canoeing
into
a whirlpool
of the motionless

caused me
to believe
I was her first
true love

deep
happiness
that moves me
turned inside out

HAUTEUR

I made
a slide
carousel
available

only
a small
bulb light
in a snail

a candle
reflected
in a gold
fish

answered
the bid
for potbellied
radiance

the
underground
economy
broadened

the shill
effect
of people
who bet

loose
discipline
got us
to this point

of say
putting out
a haywire
pamphlet

I half
laugh
at myself
for my zeal

take
a formula
and tweak
it a little

prone
to build over
what has gone
before

I feel
the stir
of arrival
and departure

a blond
lectern
stands
in between

restive
under
railway
discipline

WE'RE PRIMATES

Love
propagates
long waves
in a short rope

from Billy
on the bottom
to baby
at the top

we're primates
we climbed
as kids
innately

and
took your hand
very limply
even lately

CHELSEA SUNSET

I stumble
out of sort of
a political
headquarters

for my peers
and take
a break
on the piers

the sun
goes down
and the river
becomes fiery

obfuscation
is like oxygen
to the art
market

disclaiming art
I also
want to
disclaim merit

leaving behind
a boy
who imagined
my story

A WEIRD-LOOKING GUY

The anticipation
connected with a haircut
is disappointed
or exhausted

I'm getting to be
a weird-looking guy
reconciled to his
slide into the darkness

of a surprisingly small
inner circle
not always the best
and the brightest

I'm a regular
at a bar
and they talk about it
when I get the haircut

some fickle
forerunner of mystical
excitement awakens in them
around me

these grown men
if they are grown men
have decided
to make me their secret

their association
will have a different
meaning once I'm
done with it

it's getting
better and better
more and more enigmatic
to be part of humanity

in many ways
I'm still a family man
missing what I lost
still the nester

and I'm ready for
this fierce-looking
woman to come over
and make a play

she's on her own
like completely
what cold little hands
Jesus and Mary

she's passing her
arm through mine
in the old-fashioned
conjugal gesture

more of a change
couldn't be arranged
in so familiar
a form

all the bombs
I had to defuse
are now nuts
I can walk away from

PARISH HALL

The innocent
are so few
that two
seldom meet

romantic
and unusual
when they talk
at all

lost
in the midst
of this docile
Parish Hall

triumph
and redemption
would seem
too pointed

SAILING

Sailing
from winter
to earlier
spring

the faces
crease
in grinning
well-being

yachting
folksiness
gets
nauseating

smooth
and solid
as the sea
is tonight

a dad
in a bathing suit
a kid
in a coat

sit
or stand
as the arrangements
permit

PAUL

Paul
and Mary
play
pool

they're
at
each other's
throats

I'm
hemmed in
between
them

I get
him out
of the pool
hall

out
here
in the night
air

we will
walk till
we see
a taxi

women
make
the genetic
decisions

they
have a way
of pooling
everything

informality
matters
a great
deal

his love
is no
longer of
any value

we stand
a moment
looking out
into

the
corridor
of lower
Broadway

then
the old
historical
downtown

and
I dream
of leaving him
behind

we sit
on an ancient
concrete
bench

lighting
adequate
although
subdued

his ears
are invisible
in full
face

the air
blows cold
on our
foreheads

we look
at a plaque
and I'm
ho hum

sounds
travel farther
in the
cold air

even when
dawn
disperses
the darkness

I listen
to his quiet
and it
is a din

I talk
about Staten Island
and
Montauk

remember
another
ruinous
sunrise

an example
that's really
burning
in me

I WANT TO BE

the most occulted
deeply
invested
because

you notice
and I endure
your eyes
I want to be

known
for whipping
out pad and pen
because

the eye
prolongs
inevitable lines
I want to be

numb with
loss as the
West fades
because

I glance at
the glistening
teapot
I want to be

here or there
a nail
in the wall
I want to be

the old stone
historical
downtown
because

what are
men to water
and mountains
I want to be

paper
around wood
and varnished over
because

sex is litter
and butts
in the gutter
I want to be

one of those
indigenous
blues artists
I want to be

a blond TV set
on a three-
legged stand
because

a car with diplomatic
plates rear-ends
my taxi
I want to be

French windows
with vines
at the edges
I want to be

the figure
in a scarf
facing the ice
I want to be

a dark oak floor
polished like
a mirror
I want to be

a black cormorant
on the end
of a stake
because

every bush and tree
is twice as heavy
as usual
I want to be

those tracks
fading in the
spring thaws
I want to be

a spring imprint
of substantial
struggle
I want to be

bussed to the
self-sufficient
urban node
I want to be

what lay
beyond it
hidden by it totally
because

blasts
of fire hoses create
tableaux in niches
I want to be

a lolling smudge
of beards
and fur hats
I want to be

stationary
waters' powers
of information
because

a turn in the
stairs engulfed
the dialogue
I want to be

speaking
from under
a comforter
because

the avenue is
new and peaceful
as a fluid
I want to be

a spatial
dream soluble
in time
because

women crest
at me out of
the past
I want to be

a denizen
of this town
inside out
because

the lake
reflects
traffic lights
I want to be

a boat tied
so it can float
with the tide
because

water light
is playing
on the ceiling
I want to be

on our corner
of nocturnal
New York
I want to be

people who have
failed to achieve
the wheel
I want to be

alone listening
to the music
from the road
because

I do not
want to be looked at
even at night
I want to be

helmet paint
on the sides
of buses
I want to be

restored
when this tour
fragments
I want to be

too engaged
to incubate
an epiphany
I want to be

a lot of scattered
unexalted
culture
I want to be

a son
or daughter
upon the sofa
because

wind learns
to open
the door
I want to be

an undulating
apron of
foreground
I want to be

blurred
background
to your action
because

I see my own
house right under
my nose
I want to be

a look back
but in the
mirror too
I want to be

familiar with
architectural
wealth
I want to be

with Frank
Lloyd Wright
preoccupied in Japan
because

he's trying
to lick
himself clean
I want to be

seen talking
after long
separation
I want to be

the wherewithal
to turn
down roles
I want to be

in a foreign
setting immune
to satire
because

the final part
of America
is firepower
I want to be

chilling
memory of
the better thing
I want to be

no longer hidden
underwear
and pain
because

love
would
outweigh disgust
I want to be

calm
from the
absence of electricity
I want to be

translated and
with an
afterword
because

the problem
of boredom
is fertile
I want to be

on the stool
of rawhide
and wrought steel
because

my fingers
are loaded
with turquoise
I want to be

like starlight
dimmed by high
thin clouds
I want to be

at the end
of Route 66 in
Santa Monica
I want to be

in some
delicate undersea
installation
because

rising towers
apologize
for the mess
I want to be

simply assumed
and then
played down
because

my pet
is a fly
the size of a letter
I want to be

the rotund
and deliberate
Chinese kitty
because

my couch is
covered in
stretch velvet
I want to be

known to
write words
only afterward
because

enough calculated
fluff has
settled
I want to be

better than
modern art
by and large
I want to be

better than the best
because
quieter
I want to be

lavish
toward a person
who shows such
yearning

THE HOVERER

A melody
halts Tweety
in the middle
of a sky.

The hoverer
faces me
in all our
significance,

and I see
inquiry
and remembrance
in his glance;

we feel
relieved
as the ingredients
liquefy.

The sky
is gray,
the sun a mere
brighter blur,

and I am cast
as The
Intoxicated
Retiree,

a recluse
trying to play
with a loose
canary

in some
unused room
somewhere
on a high floor.

APPARITIONAL FIGURES

I dreamt my dad
came back from the dead
because New York
had so much work,

and I came back
as a sylvan robber
making a guest appearance
in a public park,

the botanical
rectangle
where it was a question
of victory, rebellion,

and squinting into
low September sun
to keep an eye on
my children.

PEANUT

scenes
that do not
belong
in the light

all
about
a Chihuahua
named Peanut

who would
not
vanish
quite

day
in
and
day out

(the
little
curtains
part)

a
Chihuahua
named
Peanut

hid
in
plain
sight

Peanut
busying
himself among
cartons

goes
into
a
dance

then
flashes
his
canines

unstylish
plunges
to one's
knees

to detach
him
from
bitches

in
the always
clean
hallways

kissed
by
soy
sauce

DRAFT

The wind
learned
to open
a door.

Where
is my
worthless
dreamer?

A piece
he's
required
to write

(let's
just
cut
a little bit)

has
a truly
featureless
glow.

A bough
blown
deep into
his window

lays
hold of
what is
left

but
it's just
the latest
draft.

WILL

I stoop
and creak
like
a crab

whose
shell
is
removable.

My
unmentionable
body
will

spring up
and
find
a robe.

THE SIDEWALK

People
leave
always have
always will

fail
to work
their affiliative
magic

people on
the sidewalk
around
my block

try not
to roll
the deadly
turnstile

people
employ
the language
of the leg

known
already
but not seen
until

the beloved
model
cannot
stand still

mini dust
storms kick
up in
her wake

unforeseen
women
come
to roam

vacillation
chases
the men
into place

home
where sane
women
make them

anxious
to achieve
some kind of
purchase

or
keep their
determined
distance from

accidental
slits into
exalting
vastness

LARRY'S

haughty
apartment
meant
for eternity

quiets
down so
sensations
are commensurate

Jamie
enters
and reconnoiters
his library

doorways thrown
open to an
infinite
suite

FIRE

Now
ends
the moment
of sirens

in some
nameless
Manhattan
ravines

whence
resonance
is my
fragility

a mystic
moment
after
fire

yells
I hear
as well as
utter

fall
quiet
then open out
genially

DESCRIPTION

Photography
had become
unsatisfactory
that's why

I fell in love
with women
because of
description

trying not to let
loneliness
undermine my
legacy

and sometimes the ear
fell in love
before
the eye

it could happen
like music
for which we have
a notation

rather than
like sculpture
for which there
is none

WHILE READING

Worlds
bubble up
indoors
before us

our brows
hover
over
libraries

where
abandoned
leisure
moves around

faces
crease in
grinning
well-being

and eyes
don't cease
to swing
while reading

silently
and
imagining
sound

A FEELING

Did you never
ruin your
life for
a feeling

unsure
you're liked
enough to show
your feelings

and
entertainment
arouses
your desires

that never
really gush
luxurious
as they are

BACCHANALIA

Somebody
pays a
visit to
an oasis

then
the fire
the capture
the paean

bloated
corpses
set hearts
at ease

quickly
calling
Bacchanalia
into being

the males
smell
potential
mates

o
flicker
of gonzo
recognition

a monitor
emits
camera
sights

creatures
swim
toward
exhibition

filthy face
not
without
menace

pale
blob
that probably
is male

must
wrestle
his lips
into place

Whitey
and Booty
in Stool
Refuel

eating
and singing
at the same
time

think
of nothing
but foam
and steam

SWAIN

Swain
in a ballad
half funny half sad
answers himself in a refrain

part of you
and part of me
doesn't want to let go
of what could be

the penis
well now that's a nice
surprise I'd forgotten
I had one

Swain leans his
talking skeleton head
his skull technically
close to me

the audience
has to be darkened
out of the house
into the rain

sleep with me
night after night
till it is sweet
and customary

A WILDERNESS PERIOD

Any text
was bound to succeed
in the effort
to smooth things over

but now I notice
one interesting
little critique
after another.

In the career
of a major poet
there is invariably
a wilderness period.

That remark
used to make me livid,
and now I've lived
to make it.

It would be excellent
to be old
if I traveled
toward involvement

but there is
no end
to the consequences
of wholehearted agreement.

BE A FOUND POEM

What appears to
be a found poem
is more contrived
than that.

In fact, changing
its proportions
could be
just the ticket.

*

Why have you
done this after
we have become
pleasantly tired?

The text has
become unacceptable
yet it cannot
be discarded.

HAT

Look
at that
fucking
hat

gaze
at it
as
at a sunset

there
it is
over
the trees

night
nurse
support
me please!

UNRESISTING

Stone
monuments
erode
but

clit
and tongue
get
along

a white
penis
is Pete
Rose

toes are
where
the story
is

pink
under
her
paint

a
doorway
to
duck into

in
stone
or real
on film

we are
leaning
into
curves

a
high-
minded
beauty

slides
into
bed
like a boy

radiant
not
red
but

that
you wash
is what
matters

the
subject of
shelves
of books

toils
in
regions
of curls

only
teen
milk and
honey

in
the wings
of the
theater

a woman
tucks in
her
sweater

roof
is the
only
refuge

suggestive
of
the high
sky

past
the
unresisting
teeth

COMEDIANS

Immerse yourself
in the preeminence
of the alpha
comedians

funny men
with the acumen
to justify
taking them seriously

because laughter
solidifies distaste
for the unjust
and their power

though our own
separations have
forced me to a level
of diplomacy

THE TWIN TOWERS

A tree of cracks
branches out among the bricks
but the wall
does not fall.

As the people
age in bed
tremors from the street
become unusual.

The twin towers
of the World Trade Center
become precursors
of a world at hand

where the ineffable sale
of its farmland
and of every and all people
happened.

UFO LANDS

The site
is right
on the edge
of a beach

a strong
embrace
takes the place
of language

things
change
and our feelings
become trash

I'm not
fooled by
your sticklike
appearance

give me
the sensation
of my own
resistance

the road
is repaved
where your
UFO lands

tree
rooted
in memory
of boyhood

standing
throughout
the long
open-and-shut

I'm not
fooled by
your sticklike
appearance

between
brackets
of slingshots
and canes

love is
harder
to measure
than unhappiness

I'm not
fooled by
your sticklike
appearance

MONIES

I'm
just
not used
to this slum

and
its Harvard
avant-
garde

with these
monies
to come
from

their
mother
ship in our
yard

TOWERS

You don't
understand
their
behavior

can
hover
between
past and future.

We'll
pool
our
memories.

Towers
ought
not
arise.

TREMOR

Dear
Diary,
tremor
today.

The burning
log
got
jumpy.

We
got
choreo-
graphed,

tossed
on the
earth's
crust.

IMPORTANT COLOR

I read
poets who
have no
idea

what just
happened
because
they're dead

which is
by far
the most
important color

it's what
oil
painting is all
about

CHUCKY

Pressure
from the press
brought about
hard surface roads

flyers
for readers
began to draw
protective crowds

I followed
through stretches of woods
to factories
cities

and a guiding address
where I heard
floorboards
squeeze

under cover of
no nave
no mere meeting place
for elites

but as if from an
Acropolis
peeking down
through side streets

I saw the little nook
underslung
for Chipmunk
Chucky

of strewn
light and subsuming
languageless
activity

SHOWN

Government
is fake
every week
is agreed on

what is seen
on screen
so manifestly
shown

I've seen
fuck all
might as well
have been a tree

can't
hop a flight
to a more lenient
country

EVERYTHING I DO TODAY

She jerks
him by his coat
collar, works
to bury her face in it.

I check if they move
or not,
no sign of
life all night.

The bowl
sounded
like a bell
as I urinated.

     My mother,
     taped to her
     kitchen chair
     stretcher,

     noticed
     I was no longer
     so interested
     in her.

     What
     kind of cleanup
     am I looking at
     here?

Reconciliation
came
in the time-
honored fashion,

bobbing a bit
in and out
close to one
microphone.

It's mute
so I put
subtitles on
the screen.

     I don't think
     I'll be observing
     many of those
     unities.

     My flair
     for closure
     is too serious
     for anniversaries.

     I'm this
     lifeguard
     with Kierkegaard
     open on his knees.

I watched my mother
and father quietly
from where
I lay.

Of course,
it blows
away
everything I do today.

FRIENDS DIE

I'm placed
on the
face
of Earth

and talk
to paintings
in this
house

I understand
too late
I
forget

that as
sorting grows
so does
loneliness

friends die
in my
eighties
and enemies

unforgiven
because
hate was
hit and run

intended
enjoyed
as I would
them dead

and I know
some are
waiting for
me to go

history
left me
behind
in the way

my friends die
tough
to pull off
publicly

in
pain
I'm gang-lonely
not girl-lonely

because
I am without
soldiers
yet

there
is my young
under-
pinning

loyal
at
root
level

BUT NOT YET

A lot
of rain
is in
bottles

with
both
optional
pedestals

and lips
agape
for
rainwater

but not yet
ready
for
the glare

THE ENEMY

To be
ashamed
to entertain
the enemy

because I'm acutely
aware
of their
money

all
they ask of me
is a little
more envy

and to yield
a privacy
they withhold
from me

IT'S

like
not
being
yet

before
your
gametes
met

they
say
hi
goodbye

do
you
have
a beef?

but if
you put
it
off

I
mean
come on
guy!

I.E., SKIN

We
see
a lot
about

a gun
women
might
covet

so
goes
the
tether

well
we all
wear
leather

said
Ed
Dorn
i.e., skin

some
dared
call it
Teflon

many
men
are
wary

they
carry
every
day

one man
loves
many
knives

another
lives
for
Levi's

my
memory
rockets
back to

a
novelist
I
knew

by
the
coyly
abbreviated

hand
sign
of gun
to head

HEAD ON

Hinges
I use in Maine
came from Manhattan
demolitions.

Paint
color
recalls
each apartment.

To fix this house
Christine and I
save and use
what's handy.

I could care
less about hardware
more
about war.

I've watched
a discreet
half-submerged
muskrat

duck under ice
for mussels
in Lake Sokokis.
Its pupils

reflect my headlamp
when I go out
around midnight
to exercise (exorcise) my grampa

war baby thing
by examining
the southern horizon
for a nuclear explosion.